Thérèse of Lisieux

Little Flower of Love

Also known as Thérèse
of the Child Jesus
1873–1897
Born in Alençon, France
Feast Day: October 1
Family Connection: Sisters

Text by Barbara Yoffie
Illustrated by Katherine A. Borgatti

Liguori

Dedication

To my family:
my parents Jim and Peg,
my husband Bill,
our son Sam and daughter-in-law Erin,
and our precious grandchildren
Ben, Lucas, and Andrew

To all the children I have had the privilege
of teaching throughout the years.

Imprimi Potest:
Harry Grile, CSsR, Provincial
Denver Province, the Redemptorists

Published by Liguori Publications
Liguori, Missouri 63057

To order, visit Liguori.org or call 800-325-9521.

p ISBN 978-0-7648-2289-6
e ISBN 978-0-7648-6908-2

Liguori Publications, a nonprofit corporation, is an apostolate of
the Redemptorists. To learn more about the Redemptorists, visit
Redemptorists.com.

Printed in the United States of America
22 21 20 19 18 / 7 6 5 4 3
First Edition

Dear Parents and Teachers:

Saints and Me! is a series of children's books about saints, with six books in each set. The first set, *Saints of North America*, honors holy men and women who blessed and served the land we call home. The second set, *Saints of Christmas*, includes heavenly heroes who inspire us through Advent and Christmas and teach us to love the Infant Jesus.

Saints for Families introduces the virtuous lives of seven saints from different times and places who modeled God's love and charity within and for families. Saint Thérèse of Lisieux felt the love of her family and carried it into her religious community (which included her sisters). Saint Anthony of Padua is the patron of infants and children. Saint John Bosco cared for young, homeless boys, raising them like sons. Saint Thomas More, a father of five, imitated Christ's sacrificial love and devotion to the truth until death. Saints Joachim and Anne became the grandparents of Jesus, raising Mary as a sinless disciple. And Saint Gerard Majella, the patron of pregnant mothers, blessed families with food, knowledge, penances, and healing miracles.

Which saint stood up against a king? Who became a tailor and priest? Which saint is "the little flower?" Who was known for his excellent preaching? Which saints lived before Jesus? Which saint climbed trees, did flips, and turned cartwheels? Find out in the *Saints for Families* set—part of the *Saints and Me!* series—and help your child connect to the lives of the saints.

Introduce your children or students to the Saints and Me! series as they:

—READ about the lives of the saints and are inspired by their stories.
—PRAY to the saints for their intercession.
—CELEBRATE the saints and relate to their lives.

A Family Tree

John Bosco
Champion for Youth

1815–1888
Born in Becchi, Italy
(near Turin)
Feast Day: January 31
Family Connection:
Brothers

Anthony of Padua
Wonder Worker

1195–1231
Born in Lisbon,
Portugal
Feast Day: June 13
Family Connection:
Infants

Thérèse of Lisieux
Little Flower of Love

1873–1897
Born in Alençon,
France
Feast Day: October 1
Family Connection:
Sisters

Thomas More
Faith-Filled Father

1478–1535
Born in London,
England
Feast Day: June 22
Family Connection:
Fathers

Joachim and Anne
Love for Generations

First century BC
Joachim was born in
Nazareth
Anne was born in
Bethlehem
Family Connection:
Grandparents

Gerard Majella
Guardian of Mothers

1726–1755
Born in Muro, Italy
Feast Day: October 16
Family Connection:
Mothers

We are all part of
God's family.

Louis and Zélie Martin lived in the small town of Alençon, France. They had five beautiful daughters named Marie, Pauline, Leonie, Celine, and Thérèse. Thérèse was the baby of the family. They all loved little Thérèse!

She would laugh and play with her sisters. Celine and Thérèse played in the garden. They would pick flowers and sit in the soft grass. "Flowers are so pretty. Let's take some to Mother," said Thérèse. They ran into the house and gave their mother flowers— and a big hug.

The Martin house was full of happiness and love. The family went to church together. And they prayed together. Louis and Zélie Martin knew their family was a precious gift from God. At night they would pray, "Thank you God, for our wonderful children."

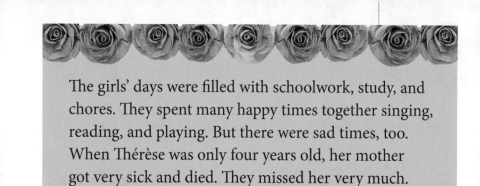

The girls' days were filled with schoolwork, study, and chores. They spent many happy times together singing, reading, and playing. But there were sad times, too. When Thérèse was only four years old, her mother got very sick and died. They missed her very much. "God will help us," Louis told his daughters.

The Martin family moved to the town of Lisieux to be near relatives. The relatives were very kind to the girls. Older sister Pauline took special care of Thérèse. "Come, little one, let me tell you about our Blessed Mother," Pauline said softly. "Can we pray, too?" asked Thérèse.

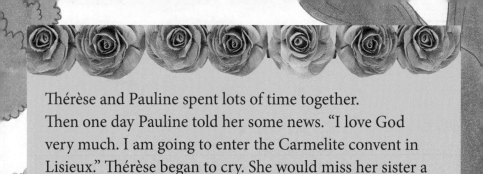

Thérèse and Pauline spent lots of time together.
Then one day Pauline told her some news. "I love God
very much. I am going to enter the Carmelite convent in
Lisieux." Thérèse began to cry. She would miss her sister a
lot! In the sad days that followed, she prayed for God's help.

Her sisters tried to cheer her up. They played games and
sang songs. Then Thérèse got sick. She had a headache
and a fever. The doctor told her to stay in bed. Her family
and friends prayed for her. Everyone wanted Thérèse to
get better.

Thérèse was in her room resting. She turned to look at the statue of the Blessed Mother. As she prayed, she saw the Blessed Mother smile. Thérèse felt so much better! "Thank you, Mother Mary! You have heard my prayers," she said.

A few years later, Marie entered the convent. She became a Carmelite nun like her sister, Pauline. Leonie joined the Visitation convent. When Thérèse told her father she wished to become a nun, too, he was not surprised. But Thérèse was only fourteen years old!

Thérèse got special permission to enter the Carmelite convent at age fifteen. This made her very happy. She was now called Thérèse of the Child Jesus.

There was a lot to do in the convent. Thérèse washed clothes, cooked, cleaned floors, and helped in the garden. Every day she grew closer to God. "I love you, Jesus, with all my heart," Thérèse prayed.

Life was not always easy. When her father became sick, Thérèse could not visit him. She felt lonely and sad. Sometimes she had trouble praying. The other nuns were older and set in their ways. If they hurt her feelings, she would smile and pray for them. She was always cheerful and kind.

Thérèse prayed for missionaries, priests, and people who did not love God. God had given her a wonderful gift: the gift of great faith. Everything she did was out of love for God. A smile, a kind word, or a helping hand was her little way of showing love.

News came to the convent that Louis Martin had died. A short time after that, sister Celine, who had been taking care of him, entered the Carmelite convent. Now the four Martin girls were together again. Pauline was the prioress (the leader) of the convent.

"Thérèse, I would like you to write a story about yourself. Write about how you love God and how you pray," said Pauline. Thérèse liked to write poems and short stories. She could share this story of love with others.

While writing her story, Thérèse became very sick. It was hard to breathe, and she was weak and tired. Thérèse had tuberculosis. "I know I will be with God soon. I shall send you a shower of roses from heaven," she whispered to the nuns at her bedside.

Thérèse, a little flower in God's great garden, died on September 30, 1897. She was only twenty-four years old. Saint Thérèse is the patron saint of missionaries, florists, and France.

Follow Thérèse's "little way":
Put love in all you do today.

Dear God.

I love you.

Saint Thérèse loved you
with her whole heart.

Help me to grow
in holiness
by trusting
and loving you.

Help me do little things
with great love.

Amen.

NEW WORDS (Glossary)

Carmelite order: A religious order founded in the twelfth century whose nuns dedicate themselves to prayer and sacrifice

Convent: A house where a group of women religious live

Missionaries: People who travel a long way to teach about Jesus

Nun: A woman who takes solemn vows and belongs to a religious order

Prioress: The leader of a group of women religious

Tuberculosis: An infection, usually in the lung. Once a serious and common disease, it is now treated with medicine.

Visitation order: A group of women religious founded by Saint Francis de Sales and Saint Jane Frances de Chantal in 1610

Saint Thérèse's autobiography, *The Story of a Soul*, has been read by millions of people around the world. It is a spiritual lesson in how to live her "little way" of trust and love.

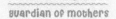